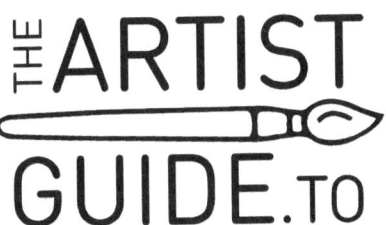

ECO FRIENDLY ART

The most comprehensive and practical guide to help you become an eco-friendly artist

SCOTT DENHOLM

Copyright © 2020 Scott Denholm

All rights reserved. No part of this publication may be reproduced, distributed, or transmitted in any form or by any means, without the prior written permission of the publisher, except in the case of brief quotations embodied in critical reviews and certain other noncommercial uses permitted by copyright law.

First Paperback Edition - Self-published May 2020
ISBN: 9798644646494
Also available as an eBook

Book design by Scott Denholm
Cover design by Scott Denholm

Scott Denholm
P.O. Box 305
Palmwoods, Queensland 4555
Australia

www.theartistguide.to

This content provided herein is simply for educational purposes. Every effort has been made to ensure that the content provided is accurate and helpful for readers at publishing time. However, this is not an exhaustive treatment of the subjects, research data and toxicology reports. No liability is assumed for losses or damages due to the information provided. You are responsible for your own choices, actions, and results. You should use all art materials within the recommended manufacturer guidelines.

TABLE OF CONTENTS

TABLE OF CONTENTS	2
HOW TO USE THIS BOOK	5
INTRODUCTION	6
WHY I BECAME AN ECO-ARTIST	8
MY STORY	9
WHAT IS ECO-ART?	19
BENEFITS OF ECO-FRIENDLY ART	21
VEGAN CONSIDERATIONS	24
PAINT	26
OIL PAINT	28
ACRYLIC PAINT	31
WATERCOLOUR PAINT	35
DIY PAINT	37
CANVAS	38
COTTON CANVAS	38
LINEN AND HEMP CANVAS	39
STRETCHER BARS	45
OTHER PAINTING SURFACES	47
ARTBOARDS	47
BAMBOO ART PANELS	50
BRUSHES	51
PRIMER/GESSO	54

SIZE	56
PALETTE KNIVES	**58**
EASELS	**60**
PAPER	**62**
SKETCHBOOKS AND ART JOURNALS	66
BRUSH CLEANER	**67**
SOLVENTS	68
MEDIUMS	**69**
VARNISHES	**70**
PRINTS/REPRODUCTIONS	**72**
GICLÉE PRINTING PAPER	72
GICLÉE PRINTING INK	74
BUSINESS CARDS	**75**
OTHER STYLES AND MEDIUMS	**76**
ENCAUSTIC	76
PENCIL DRAWING	79
PASTELS	81
DRY MEDIA FIXATIVE	83
SPRAY PAINT/GRAFFITI	84
RESIN ART	85
SUSTAINABLE PACKAGING	**86**
BUBBLE WRAP	86
STICKY TAPE	89
BOXES	90

ECO-ART SUPPLIES FOR KIDS	**91**
IN YOUR STUDIO	**92**
RECYCLING	92
LIGHTING	92
WASTE DISPOSAL	93
PAINT DISPOSAL	93
WASH WATER/LIQUID	94
RECOMMENDATIONS ON HOW TO START	**95**
THANK YOU FOR READING!	**97**
TELL YOUR FRIENDS	97
SHARE YOUR EXPERIENCE	97
GIVE FEEDBACK	97
CORRESPONDING ONLINE VIDEO COURSE	98
WORKSHOPS, RETREATS, AND SEMINARS	98
MY ART	99
REFERENCES	**100**
ABOUT THE AUTHOR	**105**

HOW TO USE THIS BOOK

Just a couple of quick notes before we get started. Although I have written this book to help guide you through the whole process, it is also quite okay for you to skip back and forth between the sections to find the specific information you might be after. I have also provided a list of source references so that if you are so inclined, you can continue your research.

This book contains URL's (links to websites), and I have provided links to specific products for ease of use. For the sake of transparency, there are no paid advertisements contained within. I do however, have working relationships with some of the brands and manufacturers, but I'm not being paid to include them. I do so because I wholeheartedly believe in the products and use them myself.

The URL's are shortened using Bl.ink URL shortener and are 100% safe. This is so that I can A, get statistics on the amount of clicks and B, so that I can repair/redirect any links by third party websites that might become dead or unusable, for example; if a product is removed from a website. Some are affiliate links.

INTRODUCTION

Hi, I'm Scott Denholm, the world's only eco-friendly artist specialising in surf/ocean scenes. I'm also a social media and content marketing consultant, part-time sports and wildlife photographer, surfer, karate black belt, environmental conservationist, and a now-published author.

First off, let me thank and congratulate you. Thank you for purchasing this book guide and congratulations for taking the initiative to become an eco-friendly artist - your first step. As Laozi so eloquently put it, "a journey of a thousand miles begins with a single step".

Whatever your motivation, I applaud you and sincerely hope that this book gives you the valuable information, guidance and inspiration that you need.

I've written this book as a valuable resource for artists to make the transition to becoming an eco-friendly artist; a transition that I made without any guides, books, websites or mentors. Needless to say, it was a long and frustrating transition and something I hope to solve for you.

My dream is to one day see an art industry that provides artists with only environmentally conscious and healthy products. And my goal with this book is to give artists the power to demand that change by voting with your purchasing decisions, one item at a time, one artist at a time. The more we as artists buy eco-friendly art materials, the more the big brands will listen and change their habits.

WHY I BECAME AN ECO-ARTIST

As an eco-friendly artist, I'm often asked why I decided to make the change from traditional art materials to the eco-friendly alternatives. It wasn't a decision that I took lightly, but once I had researched and analysed it in-depth, it was an easy choice to make. I have three key reasons for becoming an eco-artist: 1) The environment, 2) My health, and 3) Environmental awareness. You can read more about them on my website where I've written a blog that dives deeply into those three key reasons for becoming an eco-artist.

https://theartistguide.to/why-became-eco-friendly-artist/

But I also think the subtext of those three reasons is vitally important. The modernisation of the art industry plays a big role. The commercialisation of art materials (as with all industries) has led to short-term profit and greed at the expense of culture, the environment, and the community.

I feel it has resulted in the disconnect of modern artists with our subjects, the natural environment, and to an extent, spirituality.

I hope that by integrating more Earth-friendly and healthy art materials into our process, it will allow us as artists to rebuild our connection and respect to the environment and will bring us back to being the creators and custodians of our modern-day culture.

MY STORY

As a child, I grew up on the coast as well as the outback of Queensland, Australia, which was the perfect foundation for forming a lifelong love of our natural environment and native wildlife. Up until I was six years old, I lived in Bundaberg where my parents introduced me to the ocean. My earliest recollection of my interaction with the beach is swimming in the shorebreak and being pushed onto the little waves riding a boogie board at Bargara Beach by my best friend's old man. Thanks, Ian! :)

Once we moved to south-western Queensland, my childhood was full of wildlife – right in our backyard. My memory of this time was filled with catching yabbies (freshwater crayfish) and fishing for yellowbelly (golden perch) in the creek, witnessing extremely harsh and cruel weather events, stunning landscape scenery, and a few too many close encounters with bloody great big King Brown snakes. Those formative years instilled a deep connection with the land for me. Although I didn't fully understand it at the time, I always felt that the aboriginal knowledge and connection to the country had far greater meaning and substance than anything of the colonial education that we receive here in Australia - especially back in the '90s.

There are many practical uses that we can implement as a modern society that can be learnt from the ancient knowledge of our traditional owners. Implementing the full understanding of a limited subject such as the seasons that can vary greatly across a continent (rather than the acceptance of a very limited and basic four-season concept) opens up food sources, access to drinking water, photography, and eco-tourism opportunities with wildlife – just to name a few. And on a greater scale will help with the management of agricultural land that has been degraded by centuries of unsustainable practices and mismanagement of the land and resources. There is unlimited potential that resides in the wisdom, culture, and knowledge of indigenous communities that sustained their environment for millennia. Wooleen Station in Western Australia is a great example and an amazing story that is still being written.

This is when I started to become conscious of the necessity for environmental protection. It took some time for that to fully develop and for me to understand it, but it was always there. Songs by Australian artists like John Williamson also resonated with me; "Rip Rip Woodchip" is an environmental anthem that most Aussie kids who grew up in the '80s and '90s knew well. But there are a couple of lines in one particular song that really stuck out for me – even 20 years later.

The last verse of John Williamson's song titled, Ancient Mountains, which went like this:

> Now I believe we all are one
> Features and creatures in the sun
> Breathing the air we all belong
> I have a dream I can't explain
> **Wattle soldiers, making claim**
> **And paradise returns again**

John coined the term **Wattle Soldiers** as a name for environmentalists, where he envisioned people claiming large tracts of land and regenerating them to pre-agricultural/settlement conditions and repurposing them as wildlife refuges. Almost 20 years later, Steve Irwin popularised the term **Wildlife Warriors**, a name he gave to everyday people who consciously make small, everyday changes to help the environment. It was his way of including everyone in his vision. Coincidentally, Steve and Terri Irwin also purchased large tracts of land around Australia, and even internationally, for the specific purpose of revegetating, regenerating, and turning them into wildlife sanctuaries. I asked Terri about the link between John Williamson's Wattle Soldiers and Steve Irwin's Wildlife Warriors. She said it was just that, a coincidence, but she also said that it didn't surprise her that they would become friends and share very similar dreams of environmental protection.

In the days following Steve Irwin's death, John Williamson penned a song called "Wildlife Warriors - It's Time". It was a message and call-to-action from John to not see Steve's death as being in vain. Soon after, John released an album of environmental songs, including this new one, with all proceeds going to Australia Zoo's Wildlife Warriors – the non-profit arm of Australia Zoo.

I started painting with oils when I was just 10 years old, predominantly creating Australian landscape scenes. My talent was "discovered" while on a cultural school camp. I painted a tree, my dad had it framed, and that was my Mother's Day present. Mum encouraged me to pursue art/painting, so a few months later I began classes with a local artist in the tiny country town of Dulacca (meaning "emu tracks" in the local Aboriginal language).

My introduction to oil painting was very traditional and my first tutors were what I consider 'purists' in both process and technique. I'll never forget the classic oil painters smell of my tutor's studio in those early years. Little did I know that the toxic fumes from the turpentine and gum turps were doing damage to my young developing lungs. I was already asthmatic, and it certainly didn't help my condition.

During those first few years, I was encouraged by the support and feedback from my family, friends, and strangers alike. I entered art shows and won many junior and open divisions as well as selling many paintings. I was hooked, and I knew it was something I wanted to do for the rest of my life.

A few years later, my family moved to the Sunshine Coast, Queensland. At age 13, I took an interest in the ocean (OK, let's call a spade a spade... I began an obsession with the ocean). I took up bodyboarding, bodysurfing, and surfing with my school friends and completed my Surf Survival Course. Over time, my attraction to the ocean developed and became much deeper than just the thrill of riding waves. I had a love, respect and appreciation for the ocean; much the same as I did with the outback when I was younger. I also began to learn about seasonal surf and weather conditions, meteorology, marine wildlife, coastal geography, and much more.

To complement my creative nature with a career, I started a school-based apprenticeship in graphic design. One thing led to another and in 2006 (around the same time Steve Irwin passed away), I landed a great job as the Website Designer and Social Media Manager at Steve Irwin's famous Australia Zoo. During my seven years there, I became highly aware of countless environmental issues, which further amplified my interest and dedication to the environment – especially issues that affected the marine habitats that I spent so much time in and around.

During this time, I was fortunate to rub shoulders with figures like Paul Watson (Sea Shepherd), Dave Rastovich (surfer and activist, Surfers For Cetaceans), Howie Cooke (artist, activist, and co-founder of Surfers For Cetaceans) to name a few. It was through these interactions that I received an abundance of encouragement and inspiration that still impact me to this day.

Sometime during my mid-twenties, and a couple of years into my stint at Australia Zoo, I started to research and become aware of the negative impacts of the surfing industry on marine environments. Products like surf wax, surfboard foam, and neoprene wetsuits are all made from crude oil by-products with obvious negative impacts.

I figured if the surfing industry was doing this to something it says it respects and loves, then maybe the art industry that I also love is having an impact on the environment, too. Sure enough, with a little research and snooping around the internet, I found some very concerning information about not only the environment, but personal health issues as well. You can find more information about those issues later in the following chapters.

In 2009, I had a lightbulb moment. In my endeavour to always strive for positive change, I decided to combine my passions and set out to find the most eco-friendly products available. My goal was to become both an eco-conscious surfer and artist. During this time of transition, I also narrowed my focus of subject towards surf and ocean scenes, hence becoming an ocean artist. To this day (to my knowledge), I'm still the world's only eco-friendly surf/ocean artist. At least the only artist who exclusively promotes to paint surf and ocean scenes using environmentally-friendly art materials.

As mentioned, I unfortunately did not have any resources to help me through the transition. There were, and for the most part, still are, no books, websites, blogs, guides or infographics to help me, so initially, I had no idea where to start. I asked a few artist friends for their thoughts and the resounding answer was that "it's just too hard". They either thought about it but didn't want to do the hard yards or they tried, failed, and reverted to old habits and familiar products.

This wasn't good enough for me, so I persevered. That's a trait that I learnt from years of karate training and being involved in a loyal passionate music scene. They reinforced values of honour, determination, respect, and dedication that were founded by my family and parents. Perseverance is probably a bit to do with my Dutch/Scottish heritage, too!

Firstly, I started with paints. I figured that was one of the most important materials to get right before all else. Because of my partiality towards oils, I looked for better alternatives. What I learnt was that they're fairly good on their own in terms of health and environmental impact and that oil paints use natural binders such as linseed oil and walnut oil. [1] As with all paints, some pigments contain toxic heavy metals. However, most manufacturers are slowly replacing them with alternative non-toxic pigments. [2]

It is the mineral turpentine used with oils to thin the paint and clean brushes that cause all of the problems. However, traditional oils aren't effective without turps. And don't bother with odourless solvents, they just mask the issue at hand. [3] I looked into acrylics and water-soluble (AKA water-mixable oils), but, as with all types of paint, there are good and bad water-mixable oils. I spent quite a bit of money and a lot of time waiting for samples to come from different brands around the world before finally finding one that I liked (and were even better than traditional oils!). More about that later.

From there, I looked at all of my art materials, one-by-one, researching, sourcing, and testing: brushes, canvas, stretcher bars, gesso/primer, mediums, varnishes, brush cleaners, sketch paper, pencils, palettes, easels, palette knives – even down to the paper and ink that my printmaker uses to make my fine art reproductions and business cards.

Knowing what to consider when buying materials was so much more than just knowing what the product is made of. Importantly, the full lifecycle of the product can have just as much of an environmental impact as what it is made from. I also began to consider the processes involved in the production, by-products, energy consumption, packaging, health, transportation, and post-use effects. Not everything I researched had full details readily available on the internet, but most companies were more than happy to answer any questions about their product.

A good example is a canvas. The usual duckcloth cotton canvas has a much different and heavier footprint than linen or hemp canvas. This is because linen (made from the flax plant) and hemp are much more sustainable to grow and produce than cotton. More on that later.

Being eco-friendly also doesn't need to limit an artist to buying materials with a small footprint; it can be as simple as reusing and recycling. In my experience, most artists are very resourceful people and already tend to recycle household items. I'm sure you will be able to give an example of how you recycle something for your artwork, whether it be part of the artwork or part of the process.

Finally, after almost three years of researching, sourcing and testing eco-art materials, I started painting eco-friendly surf scenes with the intention to share with the surfing community. I wanted to help educate surfers, brands, and collectors about the impacts of traditional surf products and environmental marine issues. Within 12 months, I was selling my surf art worldwide to a captive audience of like-minded ocean lovers. I even entered and won a couple of art shows with my new eco-friendly surf art.

And now I've taken it a step further and here I am, seven years later helping fellow artists like you make the same move. Hopefully, you'll share the love by educating your audience about environmental issues that are relevant to you and your art!

WHAT IS ECO-ART?

Eco-art has many different forms from artist to artist depending on their needs and goals. When an artist chooses to use eco-friendly art materials over traditional art materials, they are making a conscious positive impact on the environment and even their health.

Eco-friendly art shouldn't be confused with environmental art. This is where artists use objects (not usually found in an art studio) both natural and manmade in their art. For example, some artists might create art using rubbish washed up on the beach like fishing nets, timber, bottles, etc. Others might use organic objects like driftwood, sticks, leaves, sand/dirt in their artworks.

Environmental art also deals with strong ecological issues often with political messages.

Eco-friendly artists, however, usually substitute their traditional art materials with environmentally-friendly alternatives. For example, instead of using traditional oil paint, an eco-artist would use non-toxic water-soluble paints eliminating the need for solvents.

Eco-artists may also deal with ecological and political issues within their art, but I find it is a more subtle message. I certainly do that within my own practice.

BENEFITS OF ECO-FRIENDLY ART

The benefits of eco-art are twofold. By addressing and resolving the issues with traditionally-used art materials, we'll be able to reduce, minimise, and even reverse the detrimental environmental and health impacts caused by the materials that we use as artists.

Personally, I believe the use of unsustainable resources is probably the biggest issue that needs to be addressed.

So, let's look at these issues a little more deeply so you get a good idea of what we're up against here.

The use of cotton, plastics, timber, and heavy metals should be the main focus of the materials that you should be looking to replace with sustainable alternatives. Replacing these materials should cover most, if not all, bases of materials and products used by visual artists.

Cotton = canvas
Timber = stretcher bars, palette knives, easels
Heavy metals = paint, primers
Plastic = paint, cheap palettes, single-use products

By choosing to use more sustainable products, we as artists are obviously leaving a smaller environmental footprint. Additionally, the more artists that use sustainable alternatives help encourage our favourite brands to expand their line of eco-products as well as financially support smaller brands who exclusively produce eco-friendly art supplies.

The production and waste management of toxic materials is another aspect to focus on. A lot of the products that we have used for years, and even decades, certainly have a negative environmental impact as it ends up in our waterways and landfill.

Unfortunately, there have been no studies into the overall environmental impacts of art materials at an industry, national or worldwide level. But there are numerous studies of the specific toxins within certain art materials. I have gathered some sources for further reading.

Before we delve into the products themselves I would like to point out that, all of the art materials and products mentioned here on in are of the highest professional artist quality. As a professional artist I would not use children's quality or gimmicky products, therefore I certainly will not be recommending any. These are not novelty homemade paint recipes or cheap alternatives, they are artist quality alternatives that happen to be eco-friendly - and in most cases (if not all) are of higher quality than existing products. Luckily that doesn't come at a price, as they're all competitively priced with the current products you already use.

I would also like to note that I do not claim that every product recommended in this book is 100% non-toxic, 100% environmentally safe, carbon neutral and vegan. Some are and some are merely the best available alternative to help reduce health and environmental impacts.

VEGAN CONSIDERATIONS

Additional to the sustainability and toxicity issues laid out in this book, there are animal products that need to be taken into consideration. I understand that some people won't consider this at all and some will to an extent, I would also like to cater for vegans searching for cruelty-free art materials.

In some cases, this creates a catch twenty two scenario. Where the only two options for certain products are, to use *either*, animal derived materials or synthetic/petrochemical. And until art manufacturers step up and create sustainably-sourced plant derived products this is an all too common compromise that us as artists and consumers of art supplies need to deal with. And as I will mention several times throughout, the best way for those products to be developed is by us artists insisting and putting pressure with our money and selective purchases. Afterall, they are businesses trying to make a profit like any other.

Non-Vegan Art Material Examples
Glues and binders used in sizing, paint and brushes are notably the biggest contributor to animal-based products. Using ingredients such as honey, ox gall and gelatin to name a few. Paints, especially black and dark

paints can contain charred bones. And brushes use animal hair fibres for the bristles.

As you read through my recommendations I have indicated products that are vegan. In some cases I give separate vegan recommendations. In a lot of cases however, where I haven't received enough relevant information, I haven't indicated either way. It doesn't strictly mean that it isn't.

PAINT

The paint we use across all mediums (oil, acrylic, watercolour, pastel, encaustic, art pens, ink, etc) are typically made up of two essential components 1, colourant (powdered pigment) and 2, binder medium. Both components pose issues of toxicity and unsustainability across the board. But there are some brands that are making positive changes for artists. I'll introduce them to you in the following sections. But first, I feel for you to make an informed decision, it is important to understand what it is about paint that makes it unsustainable.

Toxic Binders

The binder is mixed with pigment and is what makes each respective paint type unique. For example, linseed oil makes oil paint, acrylic polymer makes acrylic paint, gum arabic makes watercolours, etc. Unfortunately, some of these binders are far from eco-friendly or healthy for us. I'll go into detail for each paint in their respective sections below.

Heavy Metals

The pigments of all artist paints mostly come from natural mineral sources, and it's where the name of some of the more traditional colours are taken from. For example, Cobalt Blue, Naples Yellow, Cadmium Yellow and Red, Red and Yellow Ochre, Titanium White, the list goes on. Unfortunately, these are some of the same minerals (heavy metals) that are incredibly toxic to us. [5]

Some brands synthetically "mimic" these colours or remove them completely from their range and replace them with very similar - non-toxic - alternatives.

OIL PAINT

As I mentioned earlier, oil paint on its own isn't necessarily an evil product; it's the use of toxic solvents that are needed to use with them that renders them an unnecessary evil.

Toxic solvents such as mineral turpentine (turps), citric turpentine, and odourless solvents present a significant danger to your health. Particularly, breathing in the fumes causes damage to your lungs and possibly even creates many respiratory conditions. This is why all warning labels instruct to use them in a well-ventilated area. [3][4]

Also, when solvents come into contact with your skin, they are very easily absorbed into your skin and bloodstream. [3]

Water-Mixable Oil Paint
The use of water-mixable oils (also known as water-miscible and water-soluble oils) eliminates the need for solvents as they are engineered to loosely bind with water molecules, allowing them to be used with water. With water-mixable oils, water can be used in the same way solvents would be used in traditional oils; by thinning the paint for a wash or glaze technique and to wash the paint out of your brushes. Use a little

bit of soap or a non-toxic brush cleaner (I'll tell you my favourite brush cleaner in a section below).

Some people assume the oil in oil paint is a type of petroleum-based motor oil. However, the oil used is a natural nut or seed oil. Most typically- and traditionally-used is walnut or linseed oil. [1]

I haven't found a brand yet that uses cold-pressed organic walnut or linseed oil in their paint, but I'm sure it isn't too far away.

Recommended Water-Mixable Oils
wOil - Weber, an American art brand created a fully non-toxic water-mixable oil line known as wOil. Their Safety Data Sheet (SDS) showed that all pigments were harmless and the quality of this paint was very high. Unfortunately, when I last went to retrieve the SDS, I was informed that Weber had been purchased by ChartPak and the line had been discontinued. However, I have seen it for sale still and the ChartPak website has reinstated it, so there is a possibility it is back in production.

I used wOils a few times and liked them very much, but the line has only 33 colours. My only other issue is that the pigments that have been replaced - thankfully for the sake of providing a fully non-toxic line of water-mixable oil paints - have multiple pigments that make the colour less vivid and or lesser quality.

Cobra by Royal Talens
b.link/CobraRoyalTalens
This is a vegan product.

This is the brand that I have extensively used in the past. Although I only use Hydrocryl acrylics now, I used to paint with water-mixable oils and this was by far my paint of choice.

Replacing toxic pigments with non-toxic alternative, Royal Talens seem to have solved the issue that Weber wOils have with colour purity, because these are world-class paints at the same price.

They also have a much larger range of colours and mediums to help you speed up or slow down the drying process.

ACRYLIC PAINT

Acrylic paint is a whole other dynamic than oil paint. Acrylics have a relatively short history and were invented and further developed in the 1950s and 1960s during a time when various plastics were being discovered and heavily manufactured for almost everything in post-war USA and Europe. [6]

Acrylic paint is a result of the plastics boom and is derived from acrylate polymer. Acrylic paint is effectively pigment suspended in a binder of synthetic resins, (a.k.a. acrylic polymer emulsion); such binders include PVA and vinyl. A concoction of about 10 ingredients is used to make acrylic paint including anti-foaming agents. Basically, pigment mixed in plastic. [6][7]

Obviously, this creates a massive environmental issue during the full lifecycle of acrylic paint from production to canvas. It brings up issues of toxicity and large environmental footprints during manufacturing production, application, and waste management of the artist.

Their attraction as a medium for artists is their quick drying ability and the flexibility the paints afford artists within mixed media and textures.

There are very few environmentally-friendly solutions when it comes to professional artist quality acrylic paint.

There are natural paint brands that supply you with powdered pigments that allow you to mix your own binder into them, but that in itself is labour-intensive and potentially dangerous for the artist. Without the proper equipment and knowledge, fine powdered pigments are a hazard if inhaled – whether they're natural/non-toxic or not [8]. Mixing your own paint also raises issues of consistency and permanency with the end result. Mixing impure or incorrect ingredients into pigments can also lead to cracking and yellowing of paint, poor light durability, and adhesion. It's safe to say that if you don't know what you're doing, then this isn't really an option for you. However, there is a natural alternative available (see DIY Paint below).

Fortunately, there is one brand that has saved the day. Hydrocryl Acrylic Paints are a paint manufacturer based in Melbourne, Australia, who specifically produce high-end professional artist quality, environmentally-friendly, and 100% non-toxic acrylic paints.

In fact, their paint is rated to food-grade, so technically it can be safely eaten (not recommended though, it doesn't taste all that good).

Hydrocryl's pigments are a standout feature with every one of their colours a single pigment, giving them purity and vibrancy unmatched by some of the world's best paint manufacturers. Unlike all other acrylic paint brands, Hydrocryl paint does not colour shift when drying. If you've used acrylics before, I'm sure you noticed and become quite frustrated with the fact that colours dry noticeably darker than what you mixed on your palette. And as I mentioned above, Hydrocryl has eliminated heavy metals from their colour range by avoiding colours such as Ultramarine and Cadmium, instead giving artists several other very similar colour options.

For those of you outside of Australia, never fear. Hydrocryl has had a recent spike in interest and sales are now coming from the US and Europe thanks to Hydrocryl's partnership of several Colour In Your Life TV show episodes, including mine. You can buy from their online shop and they will ship anywhere in the world. I'd be forever grateful if you let them know that I recommended you when you place your order or talk to them.

b.link/hydrocryl - Use this link to get a discount.

Recommended Acrylic Paints

Hydrocryl - This is the brand that I exclusively use.
b.link/hydrocryl - Use this link to get a discount.
This is a vegan product.

WATERCOLOUR PAINT

Watercolour paints are generally a bit more environmentally-friendly because of the ease in which they're produced with natural binders. In watercolour paints, the binder is either natural gum arabic (sap from the acacia tree) or synthetic glycol. Sometimes, additives such as plasticisers (e.g. glycerin) and humectants (e.g. honey or corn syrup), are mixed in to alter various characteristics of the paint, such as consistency and durability [9][10].

Unfortunately, it can be difficult to find professional artist quality, non-toxic watercolour paints, especially in Australia. But there are a few.

Vegan Issues with Watercolour Paint
Additionally to the toxicity of watercolour paint, it can be difficult to find full colour ranges that are completely vegan and cruelty-free. This is because binders (as just mentioned above) can contain honey and ox gall. But to add to this, certain pigments contain animal products, the most prevalent is Ivory Black (also known as Bone Black) PBk9 which is made from charred animal bones. Genuine Sepia is made from squid ink and Indian Ink from crushed bugs. I have one recommendation below for a genuine series that is fully vegan and cruelty-free.

Recommended Watercolour Paints

Van Gogh Watercolours – This is the brand that I exclusively use - fully non-toxic, they avoid pigments with dangerous heavy metals.

Available in Australia at **The Art Shop**.
b.link/VanGoghWatercoloursAU
or from **Blick Art** in the US/worldwide.
b.link/VanGoghWatercolors

Here are some more great non-toxic watercolours.

Grumbacher Academy Artists' Watercolors
b.link/GrumbacherWatercolors

Micador b.link/MicadorWatercolours

Recommended Vegan Watercolour Paints

Gansai Tambin Watercolour Paints
Blick Art b.link/GansaiTambi
Jackson's Art b.link/GansaiTambiJ
Amazon b.link/GansaiTambiA

DIY PAINT

As I mentioned in the "Acrylic Paint" section, there is the option to mix your own paints, assuring their eco-friendliness because you know exactly what goes into them. However, as I have already mentioned, unless you know what you're doing, have the required equipment and location, I wouldn't recommend this.

If you do know what you're doing and wish to mix your own paints from pigment powder, there are several non-toxic options from milk paints to vegan plant-based pigments.

Natural Earth Paints have a range of vegan, non-toxic powdered pigments that, when mixed with their walnut oil, makes natural, archival quality oil paint.
http://b.link/NaturalEarthOilKit

Amazon b.link/NaturalEarthOilKitA
This is a vegan product.

CANVAS

I have previously written and blogged extensively about the merits of using a sustainably-sourced canvas.

The fibre that a canvas is made from significantly raises or lowers its level of sustainability. For painters wanting to use canvas, there are essentially three options: cotton, linen, and hemp. I will go into detail about alternative painting surfaces in another section below.

COTTON CANVAS

The issue with a standard cotton canvas (also sometimes known as duckcloth or cotton duck) is the strain that producing cotton puts on the environment. Compared to hemp and flax (linen), cotton requires large amounts of water, pesticides and herbicides, has lower yields, and requires bleaching and other chemicals in production [11][14].

Did you know: The term 'duck' comes from the Dutch word for cloth, doek.

Organic Cotton Org states that cotton is grown on just 2.5% of the world's agricultural land, yet it accounts for 16% of all insecticides and 6.8% of all herbicides used worldwide. [12]

And the WWF says,

> "It can take more than 20,000 litres of water to produce 1kg of cotton; equivalent to a single t-shirt and a pair of jeans."

[13] For more reading [14]

LINEN AND HEMP CANVAS

Alternatively, hemp and flax crops require little to no pesticides and herbicides, and much less water. They also produce higher yields per acre per year as they can be harvested after 100 days.

> "On an annual basis, 1 acre of hemp will produce as much fibre as 2 to 3 acres of cotton." [11]

The Stockholm Environmental Institute's report on the ecological footprint and water analysis of cotton, hemp, and polyester (2005) summarised that

> "In terms of material substitution, hemp had a lower impact in terms of water, energy, and the ecological footprint." [20]

Flax and hemp also have many other positive characteristics, including being a carbon-negative plant, providing nutrients to the soil (nitrogen-fixing plant), and being highly versatile which allows it to be used for many applications which results in little to no wastage including food, paper, rope, clothes, shoes, building materials, bio-diesel, bio-plastics and packaging, body care products, and many more [11].

Other than their environmental credentials, hemp and flax are an ideal canvas for many reasons. Firstly, the length and strength of the fibre make them a highly durable and rigid canvas. They're also naturally acid-free and resistant to mould and mildew, making them an ideal museum and archival quality painting surface. Hemp has been used as a painting surface for hundreds of years – even European masters used it, most notably Dutch and Flemish masters like Rambrandt and Van Gogh.

Because of the negative image portrayed on cannabis in decades gone by [11], industrial hemp has taken some time to get back to pre-WW1 production levels with cotton and nylon greatly surpassing production levels which lower costs. Hemp, and to a lesser degree, flax, is costlier to produce than cotton. But, because of the far superior quality, I exclusively use Belgian linen and hemp when requested by clients or required for extra-large canvases.

Belgian linen canvas is widely available in most art supply shops in both rolls and pre-stretched canvases. Hemp, however, will need to be sourced from a local supplier. If you're trying hemp for the first time, ask your supplier for some small samples to make sure that you get a suitable canvas.

When selecting a canvas by the roll/metre/yard/foot (depending on where you are), the weight and texture can come down to your preference. For example, fine artists who paint highly-detailed subjects usually prefer a very fine weave with little texture. And larger canvases generally require a heavier canvas to maintain rigidity and strength.

Many Belgian linen art canvases also come pre-primed with variations of coarseness and colour, just like any cotton canvas.

Size
Another element to preparing a canvas is using sizing where necessary. See the *Primer/Gesso* section for details.

Recommended Canvas

Linen

Belgian and other European-made linen is widely available as artist canvas throughout the world, both stretched and unstretched and in my opinion is currently the best type of canvas painting surface to use for many reasons. However I don't know of any brands that use non-toxic primer.

In my opinion the most eco-friendly type of canvas consists of loomstate linen or hemp canvas with FSC (Forest Stewardship Council - Forestry certified timber) sustainable stretcher bars and non-toxic gesso (both of which I mention in coming sections) by making it yourself. This ensures that you know where everything is sourced from. I understand that some people don't have the time or space to stretch their own canvases - In this case it is also possible to have custom size and material canvases stretched by professionals. Again, if you get them in loomstate, then you can apply your own non-toxic gesso to suit your needs.

Look for these brands of Linen

Libeco, Belle Arti and Claessens - Available internationally through Blick Art and Jackson's Art, they're also available in all good art supply shops. In Australia, I get mine from Chapman & Bailey and occasionally The Sydney Canvas Company.

Linen at Blick Art b.link/LinenB
Linen at Jackson's b.link/LinenJ
Linen at Chapman & Bailey b.link/LinenCB
Linen at Sydney Canvas Company b.link/LinenS

All loomstate and non-(rabbit skin glue)sized linen and hemp canvas is vegan.

Hemp

Hemp is much less available as there are very few producers making hemp canvas suitable for painting. It is also more expensive, but over time is becoming more affordable. But it is definitely out there and I regularly use it.

I recommend sourcing canvas from locally grown and processed outlets. If you think you've found something suitable, ask for a sample - most hemp wholesalers and retailers will have swatch samples available to buy for a minimal cost.

In Australia, suppliers such as **Margaret River Hemp Co**, **Hemp Wholesale Australia**.
In the US and Canada, **Bulk Hemp Warehouse** and **Rawganique**.
In the UK, **The Hemp Shop**.
In Europe, **Cavvas** and **Naturellement Chanvre**.

No doubt there are many more out there and as the stigma of hemp and cannabis is slowly removed these outlets will become more common.

STRETCHER BARS

The obvious issue with stretcher bars and frames used for stretching your canvas over is the sustainability of the timber used. For several reasons – including the carbon footprint from transport, cost of transport, and sustainability – it is almost always better to source your stretcher bars locally.

In Australia and New Zealand, artists can confidently use stretcher bars made from Hoop Pine timber (also known as Araucaria) which grows natively and is widely grown in FCS plantations.

Always check with your art retailer that the timber comes from FSC-certified suppliers. If you're unsure of the sustainability of the stretcher bars that you use, don't hesitate to simply ask your supplier.

FSC Hoop Pine is widely available and I get mine through Chapman and Bailey in Australia.

Here are some suggestions for other regions of the world.
Australia/NZ - Hoop Pine, Western Red Cedar
Europe - Nordic Pine, Scandinavian Redwood
Russia - Nordic Pine, Scandinavian Redwood
USA - Ponderosa Pine, Western Red Cedar, Tulip Wood, Scandinavian Redwood

Canada - Nordic Pine, Ponderosa Pine, Scandinavian Redwood
Mexico - Ponderosa Pine
South America - White Pine

This is a vegan product.

OTHER PAINTING SURFACES
ARTBOARDS

Artboards are a hardboard surface with a canvas or linen adhered to the surface. As with a stretched canvas, the issue with artboards is the potential use of unsustainable timber and canvas materials. From a practicality point of view, they almost always tend to warp and also need to be framed to be displayed.

I haven't used an artboard since I was a teenager, except to test the quality for this book.

Fredrix Paint Boards http://b.link/FredrixBoards

Fredrix produces a series of artboards they call "Fredrix Paint Boards" and are made using an eco-friendly blend of 100% recycled chipboard and a vegetable-based, bio-plastic core with Belgian linen (they also have a standard cotton variety).

This is a vegan product.

Hardboard Surfaces
I have started using artboards without canvas adhered for small study pieces. I initially bought several but decided to make my own to reduce costs. They are just ply board-shaped with a bevel, gessoed, and sanded surface. By making them myself, I can assure I am

using high-quality, sustainably-sourced marine ply and prime it with a gesso that I know is non-toxic.

These are great for mixed media, encaustic, and heavy paint applications.

Recommended Art Boards

Belle Arti Gesso Panels
I can recommend Belle Arti Gesso Panels. In Australia, you can get them from several places including Chapman and Bailey b.link/BelleArtiPanelsCB and the **Sydney Art Store** b.link/BelleArtiPanelsSydney.

Internationally at **Jackson's Art** Supplies
b.link/BelleArtiPanelsJ
This is a vegan product.

Also internationally, Blick Art and Jackson's Art stock several artboards that are made from sustainable materials. **Ampersand** ensure that they use FSC sourced wood for their products. Read their statement here b.link/AmpersandEco

Ampersand Available at **Jackson's Art**
b.link/AmpersandBoardsJ

Ampersand Available at **Blick Art**
b.link/AmpersandGessobord

b.link/AmpersandWood
b.link/AmpersandHardbord

This is a vegan product.

BAMBOO ART PANELS

I have used two brands of bamboo art panels as an alternative painting surface. Bamboo is another sustainable timber material. Fast-growing and easily farmed, bamboo has been counted in recent years as a great eco-friendly timber alternative. And it makes a great, solid painting surface – I've had a lot of fun painting on them.

I have found only two brands that exclusively make them as a painting surface. However, because of the lengthy process to laminate bamboo into a solid board, it is an expensive alternative. I'm hoping that the price of these products will come down with demand and popularity.

Because they are quite heavy, shipping to Australia was quite expensive.

Recommended Bamboo Art Panels

Duho Studios - California b.link/Duho
Plywerk - Oregon Washington b.link/Plywerk

As far as I know, these are the only two brands available.

This is a vegan product.

BRUSHES

For such a simple tool, brushes have a two-fold environmental impact.

Firstly, the choice of hair fibres gives artists the choice of natural hair (hog, horse, sable, etc.) or synthetic nylon hair. The obvious issue with natural animal hair is that it's centred around animal cruelty; how the hair is sourced is a point of contention for animal rights groups [16]. Vegans and artists supporting animal rights will want to avoid them.

The glue used to bind the hairs and ferrule to the handle can sometimes be made of gelatin.

However, the alternative synthetic nylon hair fibres are a plastic crude oil by-product. There are no studies on where brush hair fibres end up, but my guess is most will fall off on the painting surface and a fraction will be washed away in the brush cleaning process. Which leads me to believe that some will end up in waterways, depending on your disposal process. And depending on your location, it could very easily end up in the ocean. There are numerous studies on the number of issues with microplastics ending up in the ocean. [17][18][19]

The second issue for brushes – like so many art products – is that the handles are made from timber. So, as with everything else that I've mentioned that has timber, ideally it should be sustainably sourced. Specifically, for brushes, however, to my knowledge, there is only one brand producing sustainably-sourced timber handle brushes and that's an Australian brand called Micador.

Recommended Brushes

Micador - FSC timber handle brushes
b.link/MicadorBrushes

Ideally, I'd like to see brushes that feature both FSC timber handles and sustainable/cruelty-free hair – possibly made from a biodegradable material or even a natural material such as bamboo. I know that there are bamboo hair makeup brushes, so I'm curious about the application of bamboo for art brushes.

I also have some house painting brushes that are made from bamboo handles, recycled aluminium ferrules, and recycled synthetic hairs. I found these at the local hardware store, so keep an eye out for those.

Recommended Vegan Brushes
Unfortunately, I can't find information on the source of the timber used to create the handles for the following

brushes, but I am assured they are all vegan in both hair type and glue.

Jackson's Art have a whole section dedicated to vegan-friendly brushes. b.link/VeganBrushes

PRIMER/GESSO

Traditionally, gesso is a mix of an animal glue binder (usually rabbit skin glue), chalk, and white pigment used to coat rigid painting surfaces. However, modern gesso (acrylic gesso - technically not really a gesso) is formulated to prime a wider variety of surfaces — including non-rigid surfaces like a canvas — with an acrylic polymer medium-like latex and other chemicals to make it flexible.

Note: Modern acrylic polymer-based gessoes are non-absorbent, making it incompatible with media such as egg-tempura. The use of modern mediums and some chemicals render gesso toxic and, therefore, an environmental and health risk.

Fortunately, there are several brands that are creating non-toxic gessoes.

Recommended Gesso/Primer

Tri-Art Sludge Gesso
Canadian art brand, Tri-Art's Sludge Gesso is a by-product created from the waste of their acrylic paint production. This is an idea and technique that I believe all paint manufacturers should be exploring to create sustainable production methods and products. Just a note, this gesso is a bit runnier than most modern

gesso and is a more natural off-white colour. It's by far my favourite gesso!
Blick Art b.link/TriArtSludge
Amazon b.link/TriArtSludgeAmzn

Natural Earth Gesso

Natural Earth Paints have created a kit that allows you to mix the world's first (and possibly only) eco-friendly + vegan, artist-quality gesso. My only issue with this is that making it yourself invites inconsistencies and impurities. There is no way to know the longevity and integrity of it. My hope, of course, is that it is successful.
b.link/NEPEcoGesso
Amazon b.link/NEPEcoGessoA
This product is vegan.

National Art Materials Gesso

Widely available in Australian art shops, this is a non-toxic gesso with great tooth and is very affordable.

Holbein Acrylic Gesso

Holbein also claims to have an eco-friendly acrylic gesso, but their SDS report show low (not non) toxicity and uses the standard acrylic polymer. I have a feeling their claim is specifically about the packaging and not the ingredients of the gesso.

SIZE

As mentioned above, sizing is necessary in the preparation of canvases for some disciplines. Sizing is a layer placed between the canvas and the primer and paint. The size acts to isolate the fabric/surface from subsequent applications of primer and oil paint preventing canvas rot. This is specifically necessary in oil painting because over time the linseed oil rots away canvas fibres.

If you're unsure when to use size, follow this great information sheet by Golden. b.link/GoldenInfoSheet

Traditional Size
Traditional sizing is made from rabbit skin glue (yes, actual rabbits). This is obviously problematic for vegans and anyone conscious of not wanting to harm animals. The other reason why rabbit skin glue isn't the most suitable skin is because over long periods of time, art conservationists say, rabbit skin glue flexes in varying humidity. So over time the glue will expand and shrink causing aged oil paintings to crack and over time flake off. [22]
This extensive study by Marion F. Mecklenburg of the Smithsonian Institute goes into great detail about the effects of humidity on various painting surfaces, size, gesso and even how different pigments react. It's a very interesting but technically-demanding read.

Modern size

Modern sizing has all but eliminated the humidity issues. However, it is just a variation of preto-chemical derived PVA glue and contains toxins ammonia and formaldehyde as preservatives.

Natural Earth Paint has created a vegan, non-toxic, plant-based size from Methyl Cellulose. However, my understanding is that Methyl Cellulose, like traditional rabbit skin glue, is hygroscopic, meaning that it absorbs atmospheric moisture, which over time could behave the same way as rabbit skin glue. Having said that, at this time there is no evidence to support either way and I am very grateful that a brand has at the very least stepped up to provide an eco-friendly alternative. I'm sure it will be further developed over time to become more suitable too.

Recommended Size

Natural Earth Paint Vegan Size b.link/NEPSize

PALETTE KNIVES

In most cases, the handle of a palette knife is made from timber. There are some brands that make the handle from plastic and some that are made entirely of steel, however, I've found these harder to grip.

As with all timber products that I've mentioned so far and will mention throughout this whole book, the timber needs to be sustainably sourced.

One Australian brand, Art Spectrum, does just that. The timber used for their palette knife handles is sourced from decommissioned olive trees in Italy. This is a great example of a sustainable by-product. The trees are a couple of hundred years old and once they stop producing olives, they would normally be destroyed and replaced with new trees. Luckily though, the olive tree timber has some great qualities about it, including that it is hard, non-porous and will not absorb flavours, odours or bacteria making it the perfect timber for such use.

Personally, I used Art Spectrum palette knives from the age of about 12 through to 30 and had the same two or three knives that whole time. They eventually broke but took more than 15 years before that happened! I tried some other brands for a couple of years, however, they were of inferior quality and kept breaking, prompting me to go back to Art Spectrum. I've had my three current knives for about three years now and will never go to another brand.

Recommended Palette Knives

Art Spectrum Palette Knives b.link/ASPaletteknives
It is difficult to find these online, but Art Spectrum have distributors worldwide, so you will be able to order them through a local store. Luckily they last for years.
This product is vegan.

EASELS

Easels are made almost exclusively from wood. So, the certification and sustainability of the wood used are important when choosing an easel. The most common timbers used for easels are lightweight hardwoods. Beech and bamboo are most common and are well regulated. As with other timber products I've mentioned, be sure to ask the retailer or maker if they know where the timber is sourced from. Makers with nothing to hide will be transparent and even proud to share that their timber is sustainable.

I have both beech and bamboo easels and both are incredibly tough and will likely last for decades.

Recommended Easels

Mabef
Mabef are one of these brands that are transparent. They use Italian Beech wood and show their FSC certification on their website. These are very well made and extremely durable easels that I can highly recommend. b.link/MabefEasels

Blick Art b.link/MabefEaselsB
Jackson's Art b.link/MabefEaselsJ

This product is vegan.

Bamboo

Jasart make a line of bamboo easels, but they do not seem to have any online retailers. In Australia, you can find these easels in Eckersley's and most big art supply shops. I suspect the same for the rest of the world too.

PAPER

As with wood products, paper products highlight the issue of sustainability. Additionally, however, the production of paper adds more issues to the fold. Chemicals, bleaching, and a lot of water are used to make paper, so choosing one that minimises those is important.

The thing you're looking for in paper is acid-free, chlorine-free, and post-consumer sourced materials. Also, paper doesn't have to be made of timber; in my opinion and experience, the best paper is made from rag (cotton) and other natural fibres such as hemp.

For me, there are two standout brands to choose from.

Khadi
This is the one that I mainly use and recommend. Very nice paper, more of a traditional/handmade feeling but very high-quality professional artist paper. Khadi specialise in artist paper for many uses including drawing, watercolour, and painting. It is widely available in Europe and worldwide. Online it is available from Jackson's Art.

Produced in a highly sustainable manner, Khadi paper is raising the bar for eco-friendly paper.

Read more about their paper and environment here:
b.link/KhadiAbout | b.link/KhadiEco

Recommended Drawing and Watercolour Paper

Khadi Paper
Jackson's Art b.link/KhadiPaperJ

*Vegans please note - Khadi use gelatin as their internal and external size. I have listed some vegan-friendly paper below.

Fabriano
Fabriano also sustainably produces high-quality artist paper for many mediums and uses. Their paper is widely available in Europe and worldwide. They are also available online from Jackson's Art. Fabriano is also vegan-cruelty free paper.

You can read about their environmental credentials on their website here: b.link/FabrianoEco

Fabriano Paper
Blick Art b.link/FabrianoPaperDB
Jackson's Art b.link/FabrianoPaper

Sustainability Certification of paper
A side note to the certification of paper: Unfortunately, at this present time, there is no independent, third-party

certification system that traces and verifies the source of non-wood pulp paper. The fact that most fibres used to make eco-friendly paper come from plants such as bamboo, hemp, jute, lokta, and mulberry to name a few – all of which are commonly known as grasses and smaller plants, and not trees. So, the FSC certification system doesn't apply. There is an FSC scheme for bamboo, but that is currently for timber-based products such as furniture and flooring.

Vegan Paper
Sizing is used to ensure liquids and pigments dry on the surface of paper. Most manufacturers (especially of watercolour paper) tend to use gelatin as a size, which renders that paper non-vegan. As I mentioned in the vegan section earlier, some manufactures counter this by using synthetic size, however, as also explained earlier, this can mean the use of plastic-derived materials making it not eco-friendly.

Recommended Vegan paper

Fabriano
As mentioned above. Links to paper sheets and sketch pads above and below in their respective sections.

Canson Moulin Du Roy Watercolour Paper
Sized with starch. Also acid free and made without bleaching agents.

Jackson's Art b.link/Moulin
Blick Art b.link/MoulinDB

Strathmore Papers

Plant-based and synthetic sizing in the manufacturing of nearly all of their papers, excluding the 500 Series Gemini Watercolour Paper.

Blick Art b.link/StrathmorePaper
Jackson's Art b.link/StrathmoreJ

SKETCHBOOKS AND ART JOURNALS

The two paper brands above produce amazing quality artist sketchbooks and art journals. My favourite multimedia art journals that I have used for years and are an absolute pleasure to use – not to mention, very aesthetically pleasing – are Khadi's handmade bound sketchbooks. They come in two textures, smooth and course, and a few different sizes.

Recommended Sketchbooks and Art Journals

Khadi
Jackson's Art http://b.link/KhadiSketchBooks
This is the paper I used for the cover artwork of this book.

Fabriano
Blick Art b.link/FabrianoSketchDB
Jackson's Art b.link/FabrianoSketch

This product is vegan.

BRUSH CLEANER

Traditional brush cleaners are harsh, toxic solvents. But there are a few non-toxic options becoming available.

Of all my eco-friendly art products, this is my favourite find. I exclusively wash my brushes with The Masters® Brush Cleaner and Preserver. As far as I'm concerned, this is the best brush cleaner available and the only one you'll ever need. I have brought some badly-damaged brushes back from the brink using Masters and in my experience, it greatly lengthens the use you get out of your brushes. Not only that but after cleaning brushes with it, it makes them feel almost new again each time. This sounds like a paid endorsement, but I assure you it's not – I just love it that much.

Recommended Brush Cleaner

The Masters® Brush Cleaner and Preserver
You can get it in most art shops worldwide and is probably best-priced on Blick Art online. Australian's please note, this product in Australian art shops is more than double the online/US price.

Blick Art b.link/MastersB
You can also find it on **Amazon**
Large b.link/MastersALrg Medium b.link/MastersAMed
This product is vegan.

SOLVENTS

Solvents are the biggest issue with health and environmental concerns for artists [3]. Solvents contain very harsh chemicals that are unsafe, and I do not recommend using traditional solvents at all. However, if you do still want to use traditional oils or water-mixable oils with solvents, there are a limited number of natural, non-toxic products available.

The Natural Earth Paint company in the USA also makes a few products, with one solvent in particular possibly being the best option on the market.

Eco-Solve
Eco-Solve by Natural Earth Paint is a non-toxic, all-natural professional paint thinner. You can read about their product and buy it here:
Natural Earth Paint b.link/NEPSolvent
Amazon b.link/NEPSolventA
This product is vegan.

Maimeri Eco Cleaner
This is a non-toxic, non-hazardous, eco-friendly brush, palette, painting knives, and mixing bowl cleaner. It is an ammonia-free, odourless, slightly foamy and dilutable with water and poses no threat to your health or the environment. It is even packaged in a recyclable, PET plastic bottle. b.link/Maimeri
This product is vegan.

MEDIUMS

As I mentioned in the oil painting section above, the oils in oil paint are generally walnut or linseed oil. It is quite easy to avoid toxic mediums for oil painting as many of the current top brand options are just walnut or linseed oil with non-organic additives and preservatives that render them unsafe. By choosing brands that make non-toxic oils, you can easily avoid any toxic materials.

Recommended Painting Mediums
All recommended mediums are vegan.

Walnut Oil - Natural Earth Paint
Natural Earth Paint creates an all-natural walnut oil for oil painting medium.
b.link/NEPWalnutOil
Amazon b.link/NEPWalnutOilA

Gamblin Solvent-Free Oil Mediums
Blick Art b.link/Solvent-FreeMediumsB
Jackson's Art b.link/Solvent-FreeMediumsJ

Linseed Oil

Eco-House - Light Refined Linseed Oil
b.link/LinseedEco
Old Holland - Windmill Cold Pressed Linseed Oil
b.link/LinseedWindmill

VARNISHES

Unfortunately, this is an area lacking in high-quality products that are fully non-toxic, especially if you're looking for low gloss or low sheen varnishes for acrylic and other non-oil mediums. The best that can be found is low VOC. There are some water-based low VOC varnishes, but that's the best I have found. It seems we're waiting for the manufacturers to create one.

The best I have found are low-toxic, turpentine-free and low odour varnishes. There are wax varnishes but I have never used them and they are made from plastic.

Eco-House, a Canadian art brand, has a range of mediums and varnishes that are made from natural organic ingredients and are safe to use, but not fully non-toxic. Their Damar Varnish gives a semi-gloss protective finish coat to well-dried oil and water-mixable oil paintings and is made with their Xtra Mild Citrus Thinner and linseed standoil, rather than the normal turpentine mixture of other brands..

I rarely use varnish but when I do, I personally use a low VOC spray varnish by Australian art brand, **Micador**. Usually in a satin finish.

Recommended Varnish

Eco-House Damar Varnish
b.link/EcoDamarVarnish
This product is vegan.

Micador
b.link/MicadorVarnish

Just days before this book was published, **Natural Earth Paint announced they have developed over 2 years a new plant-based non-toxic varnish. This varnish is a high gloss liquid that seems to me to mimic the look of renaissance period paintings.

Although I personally don't like the look of high gloss varnish (I rarely use varnish), I will buy some and try it out for myself. Hopefully this is the beginning of more brands coming onboard with eco varnish.

b.link/NEPVarnish
This product is vegan.

PRINTS/REPRODUCTIONS
GICLÉE PRINTING PAPER

When getting reproductions and giclée prints of your work, be sure to consider the sustainability of the paper that your artwork is printed onto. Ask your printmaker if they stock cotton rag and/or sustainably-sourced papers. As with drawing and watercolour paper, the paper that your artwork is printed to should strive to be acid-free, chlorine-free, and sourced from post-consumer materials. Again, paper doesn't have to be made of wood-pulp – rag (cotton) and other natural fibres such as hemp are, in my opinion, superior to timber paper.

Also, as mentioned in the above paper section, unfortunately, at this present time, there is no independent, third-party certification system that traces and verifies the source of non-wood pulp paper. The fact that most fibres used to make eco-friendly paper come from plants such as bamboo, hemp, jute, lokta, and mulberry to name a few – all of which are commonly known as grasses and smaller plants, and not trees. So, the FSC certification system doesn't apply. There is an FSC scheme for bamboo, but that is currently for timber-based products such as furniture and flooring.

There is one specific brand that my printmaker stocks that I can highly recommend.

Moab Entrada Cotton Rag

In general, the Moab (and mother company, Legion Paper) pursues some ideally sustainable practices. Their mills and offices are run on 100% renewable wind power; none of their papers have been bleached; papers are handmade, thus reducing energy usage; compliant to internationally-recognised environmental management system (EMS) standards, and; are 100% tree-free using various other fibres to produce their stunning papers.

GICLÉE PRINTING INK

The ink considered for printing purposes is quite important because printer ink is a toxic blend of petroleum products and pigments.

Still considered to be in the infancy of the technology, there are high-quality, plant-based inks that some printmakers use. There are non-toxic inks, mostly soy-based and some other vegetable-based inks, that feature great pigmentation and colour fastness. However, because giclée prints are considered the highest quality of all printing and the fact that soy-based inks – specifically for giclée reproductions – are considered early technology, means they are not widely used for this purpose.

Soy-based inks, however, are perfect for the lesser-required archival-quality types of printing such as newspapers, magazines, brochures, and, of course, business cards. See the section below.

BUSINESS CARDS

As with your giclée reproductions, you should heavily consider recycled and/or sustainable paper and soy-based inks for your business cards. Simply for the fact that, as I just mentioned above, your business cards do not require the highest archival qualities; they can be printed with no hesitation using soy-based inks.

All major and good printshops and business card printing agencies will be able to give you these options. I specifically have my business cards printed on recycled cotton rag paper with soy ink and they look, feel (and smell) amazing.

OTHER STYLES AND MEDIUMS

ENCAUSTIC

Encaustic painting is an interesting medium when considering environmental, vegan and personal health concerns. Of course, the pigment is the same as oil, acrylic, and watercolour, however, it is bound using wax. As this is the case, most encaustic artists blend their own pigments with raw pigment powder and wax. The wax of choice for most encaustic artists is beeswax, which is natural and non-toxic, however, for artists who would prefer vegan wax, there are plant and soy options available.

Scientists partnering with art professors have been working to "modify the soy molecules to make them behave like beeswax with improved cohesiveness." [24] Thus making the wax to "perform more like traditional encaustic waxes for stability and archival quality". It is also a cheaper alternative to the traditional beeswax. Read the full research paper here [25]

The other issue that encaustic artists contend with is the process of heating the wax. Using blowtorches and other heating devices consumes a lot of energy. This is also where using natural wax is important, too – so as not to release dangerous chemicals from the wax in the heating process. For this reason it is important to avoid petroleum based waxes such as microcrystalline and paraffin wax.

Recommended Encaustic Wax, Grounds and Mediums

Art brand **R&F** are a reputable brand championing research into best practices and materials and consequently creating non-toxic and also vegan encaustic materials.

A note about their gesso - it is an acrylic/water-based gesso, but safety sheets show it is completely non-toxic (and free of rabbit skin glue making it vegan too) - very important for encaustic painting.

In Australia, you can get **R&F** beeswax, soy wax and damar resin from **Chapman & Bailey**.
b.link/EncausticCB

Soy Wax *Vegan
Blick Art b.link/SoyWax
Amazon b.link/SoyWaxA
This product is vegan.

Beeswax
Blick Art b.link/BeeswaxB
Amazon b.link/BeeswaxA

Encaustic Gesso
Jackson's Art b.link/EncausticGessoJ
Blick Art b.link/EncausticGessoB
Amazon b.link/EncausticGessoA

Medium
Jackson's Art b.link/EncausticMediumJ
Blick Art b.link/EncausticMediumB
Amazon b.link/EncausticMediumA

Damar Resin
Blick Art b.link/Damar
This product is vegan.

PENCIL DRAWING

Pencils have a twofold issue with the timber and colour toxicity. Luckily enough, they are widely produced with non-toxic colours and there are several brands producing them with FSC sustainable timber.

Vegan Issues

A lot of pencils, unfortunately, are not vegan. Animal products like shellac are used in binders, glues and wood finish to make pencils. Fortunately, I can highly recommend Faber-Castell.

Recommended Art Pencils

Faber-Castell

Faber-Castell has made and implemented a social and environmental commitment to using only FSC timber throughout their whole range. They're also completely non-toxic, vegan and cruelty-free.

Drawing Pencils
Jackson's Art b.link/Faber-CastellPencilsJ
Blick Art b.link/Faber-CastellPencils

Watercolour Pencils
Jackson's Art b.link/Faber-CastellWCPencilsJ
Blick Art b.link/Faber-CastellWCPencils

In Australia, **Micador** makes non-toxic, FSC timber pencils artists and children.
Micador FSC Pencils b.link/MicadorPencils

PASTELS

Artist pastels, also known as soft pastels and (mistakenly) chalk pastels, share the same issue as paint. The pigment is made from, and in the same way as, paints. The only difference is that they are suspended in a different binder (usually clay such as kaolin and gum arabic) that obviously hardens the pigment into a stick.

Another issue with pastels is that they release a very fine dust when they're being used that is very easily inhaled.

And as with all dry media, pastels sometimes require a spray fixative to adhere the pigment to the surface or to rework over sections of paintings. Aerosol spray fixative is much like varnish and solvents and highly toxic. However, there is one non-toxic spray fixative available. See the **Dry Media Fixative** section.

There are a few companies that produce non-toxic pastels and one, in particular, in the highest standard of artist pastels.

Recommended Pastels

Royal Talens - Rembrandt Soft Pastels
This line of pastels use natural binders and kaolin.

Blick Art b.link/Pastels
Jackson's Art b.link/PastelJ
Amazon b.link/PastelA

This product is vegan.

DRY MEDIA FIXATIVE

As mentioned above, dry media/mediums such as pastels, charcoal, pencil, Conté, graphite and more sometimes require a spray fixative to adhere the pigment to the surface or to rework over sections of paintings. Fixative is also used as a sealant for the final artwork to be protected against smudging and even to eliminate the need for glass when framing.

Aerosol spray fixative is much like spray varnish and is highly toxic. However, there is one non-toxic spray fixative available.

Recommended Dry Media Fixative

Spectrafix
Spectrafix is the only non-toxic fixative on the market. It is odourless and made from natural milk casein (milk protein).

Jackson's Art b.link/SpectrafixJ
Blick Art b.link/SpectrafixB
Amazon b.link/SpectrafixA

SPRAY PAINT/GRAFFITI

Spray paint is one of the most toxic and environmentally unsustainable painting mediums. Spray cans require certain compounds and gasses to pressurise and release the paint combined with the binder which is almost always petroleum-based.

Street art brand, **Ironlak** have created a water and alcohol based spray paint with the alcohol made from sugarcane. Petroleum and solvent-free, their **Sugar Aerosol Paint** contains far fewer Volatile Organic Compounds (VOC's) which significantly reduces the health and environmental impacts of spray paint.

This is by no means the saviour that has completely solved the issue - gasses such as butane are still used to release the paint under pressure - it is merely a better option. Ironlak themselves have also acknowledged that this product is a (significant) first step to a truly non-toxic and environmentally sustainable solution and they are committed to continually improving those aspects of the product. In light of that, Ironlak still recommends wearing gloves and a mask.

Recommended Spray Paint

Ironlak Sugar
b.link/SugarPaint

RESIN ART

Resin art is created using epoxy resin, usually in a two part system containing resin and hardener. Epoxy resin is of course a petrochemical plastic mixed with several chemicals, including Bisphenol A (BPA) and formaldehyde. Meaning this medium is very much toxic and or carcinogenic/mutagenic.

I have studied the SDS sheets of a couple of resin art brands that claimed their resin to be non-toxic, but I found those safety sheets missing critical - and in my opinion absolutely necessary - information.

I cannot recommend any resin art brands or even the medium in general. But if you are really wanting to, flow painting will be a better option. For example, you can use Hydrocryl acrylics with their Flow Promoter, but I do realise this is a very different alternative.

Until bio-resins (plant-based) are made to be a suitable binder for pigment, there is no safe, non-toxic solution.

SUSTAINABLE PACKAGING
BUBBLE WRAP

Unfortunately, using plastic derived packaging materials is an unnecessary evil. But we can minimise our footprint in a couple of different ways.

The one important piece of advice I can give you is to avoid bubble wrap products that are marketed as degradable or biodegradable. These products are technically known as oxo-degradable and oxo-biodegradable and are made from plastic polymer materials that are modified with chemicals to speed up the degradation process through exposure to UV light, heat and oxidation. There are several issues with this technology.

1. They are still made from polymer resin plastics and once broken down, turn into micro-plastics that end up in our waterways and oceans and eventually our food and water sources - which is now a widely studied and documented environmental issue. A new global study by WWF and the University of Newcastle in Australia, revealed that we might be ingesting as much as 21 grams of micro-plastic per month found in our food, water, and air. [21]

2. Infact, a study commissioned by the European Union found that there is a risk that the use of "oxo-degradable" additives will accelerate the

process and "accumulating amount of microplastics in the environment, especially the marine environment." [22]
3. If this material decomposes underground without oxygen, it releases methane which is 25 times more harmful than CO2. [22]
4. Although there is little testing and little research, the EU is concerned that the added oxidation chemicals could be toxic and leach into soil and waterways. [22]
5. The term "bio" should never be used for materials derived from plastic. It is incredibly misleading and I personally believe that advertising standards need to catch up and not allow this to happen. The only time "bio" should be used is when the base materials are from organic sources, such as cornstarch and is fully compostable.

So, the question becomes, what should we use and do about it?

At this stage, the best alternative is to avoid oxo-degradable bubble wrap and use 100% recycled bubble wrap - which is quite easy to source. Here in Australia, we have a large hardware store chain called Bunnings that sells bubble wrap made from 100% recycled materials. And always make sure to encourage the recipient to reuse or recycle it.

Fortunately, there are better alternatives and technology coming to the market that will hopefully become affordable for consumers in the not-too-distant-future. Natural bio-plastic resin is being made from peanuts, cornstarch, hemp resin and I've even seen packaging made from mushrooms. Cornstarch is most widely used at this stage. Hopefully by the next update of this book, I'll be able to recommend a specific product. The best thing you can do as a consumer is make sure manufacturers and retailers know that there is a demand for alternative sustainable bubble wrap.

Another thing you can do if you're transporting paintings a short distance is avoid using bubble wrap altogether use blankets and towels. Just make sure they're washed, as the natural oils from our skin which we sweat out while sleeping are slightly acidic and could have long term effects on a painting.

STICKY TAPE

Avoiding single-use plastics is a very good way to make your packaging and art process more environmentally-friendly. Sticky tape is one of those single-use products that I always wish wasn't necessary. Luckily enough, there are a couple of great options.

Packaging giant, **Tesa**, now has a range of eco-friendly sticky tape that is made from recycled materials and bio-based resources and does not use solvents or bleaching agents for the adhesive. Find out more on their website b.link/TesaTape

But my favourite option - especially for creatives - is Australian sustainable packaging brand **noissue**. Their tape is FSC certified and printed using soy ink. Why do they need soy ink you ask? Because the best part about their tape is that it's customisable. You can add you logo, your art... anything. This is a little touch for branding. b.link/NoIssueTape

BOXES

When boxing your artwork for transport, use recycled cardboard boxes and make sure you encourage the receiver to break down the box and put it into their recycling bin or to reuse the box again.

For large paintings, the best place to look for large boxes is at department stores that sell very large TVs or bicycles. The owner of my local bicycle shop is kind enough to put discarded boxes aside and allows me to periodically take what I need; these are usually the perfect shape and is very strong, rigid cardboard.

ECO-ART SUPPLIES FOR KIDS

There are many eco-friendly options for children's art supplies. Most non-toxic paint is catered to the 5-15-year-old child market. There are also some vegan kits made from soy and vegetable pigments, but please be careful of DIY mixing kits. Even though these are non-toxic, the extremely fine-powdered micro-dust of the pigment is easily inhalable, so please be incredibly careful with kids mixing powdered pigments. Using caution and small scoops will minimise dust.

Natural Earth Paint
b.link/NEPChildrensPaint

This product is vegan.

IN YOUR STUDIO
RECYCLING

Being eco-friendly doesn't need to limit an artist to buying materials with a small environmental footprint; it can be as simple as reusing and recycling. In my experience, most artists are very resourceful people and already tend to recycle household items. I'm sure nearly all of you will be able to give an example of how you recycle something for your painting and art practice already – whether it be part of the artwork or part of the process.

For example, I use old clothes for rags, jars for holding brushes, and old glass chopping boards for palettes. I also buy canvases at thrift stores (known as op shops in Australia) and use the canvas for study pieces. If I find a good-quality stretched canvas, I will salvage the stretcher bars and stretch my own Belgian linen over it. I also reclaim old surfboards to paint on.

LIGHTING

For some artists, lighting your studio uses a lot of energy and is costly on your power bill. Consider using LED lighting, the technology is rapidly improving and giving consumers much more energy and cost-efficient lighting solutions. LED lights also radiate little to no heat from the bulb, making your studio much more comfortable in warm weather.

WASTE DISPOSAL

Waste disposal is a tricky area. Proper disposal allows us to keep as much of what we use from ending up in the soil and waterways. Whether we're using non-toxic products or not, it's still a good idea to thoughtfully dispose of your paint and wash water. Here are some techniques that I use that I will share with you.

PAINT DISPOSAL

Any excess paint that I remove from my palette is scraped into a small container. That container eventually goes into the bin. However, before I get to that point, I do a few things to minimise the amount of paint that I waste. Firstly, I only ever put as much on the palette as I know I will use. Knowing how much you're going to use comes with practice, but it always helps to be conservative (you can always just mix up more paint). It's much better than the alternative, which is, if you have spare paint left over, trying to put it into sealable containers to use in another session.

If I need to keep my palette overnight or for another session, putting paint in the freezer will slow its drying time. Be sure to keep it in an airtight container or seal it with a biodegradable cling wrap. There are cornstarch and beeswax wraps and some new technology being made all the time, so try to avoid plastic cling wrap where you can.

WASH WATER/LIQUID

If you use water (like I do) to wash your brushes and equipment, there is a technique that you can use to stop dirty paint water from needing to be disposed of.

I wash everything in a bucket, then once finished, I pour the water into a shallow container and then put it outside. Eventually, the water evaporates, leaving the pigments and other materials on the bottom of the container. I repeat that process after every session and reuse that container, eventually disposing of it in the rubbish.

RECOMMENDATIONS ON HOW TO START

If, for financial restrictions, you cannot start or replace your whole painting kit with the eco-friendly recommendations that I've made, then just start by replacing single items as you need them. This is mostly how I went about it in the beginning. Of course, if you are in a position to be able to get everything at once, then, by all means, go for it – more power to you!

The good thing about replacing items as you need them is that there is no right or wrong order or way to go about it. One product, for example, brushes, doesn't rely on another product being replaced at the same time. All of the items I've recommended can be used with your existing kit. If you buy new eco-friendly brushes, they will still work with your current paint. If you buy eco-friendly linen canvas, that will still work with your existing paint, brushes, gesso, etc.

The only thing I'd be wary of is using multiple brands of acrylic paint at the same time and also using water-mixable oils with normal oils. You might run into some incompatibilities with drying and possibly molecular/chemical inconsistencies between brands of paint that could cause issues with the structural integrity and longevity of the paint. So, for example, I wouldn't go mixing a "flow" acrylic of one brand with a "structure" acrylic of another brand.

With that said, if you're an oil painter who uses acrylic paint as an underpainting, I can highly recommend Hydrocryl acrylics as an underpainting.

When it comes to replacing your paints and budget is a factor, I would recommend first getting a starter pack. That gives you the basic but essential colours and from them, you will be able to mix almost any colour you need. If you're learning to paint, limiting your colours is a great way to learn about and understand colour mixing and colour theory. From that starter pack, you can then slowly acquire more colours as you need them.

THANK YOU FOR READING!

Well, that's it! Thank you so much for reading my first book! I really do hope that you have gained some valuable knowledge. With this newfound knowledge, you are now empowered to help me put pressure on art brands to offer us only environmentally- and health-conscious art materials.

TELL YOUR FRIENDS

If you've loved this book and found it useful then please tell your art friends all about it and send them to my website or to where you purchased it! The more artists this book reaches, the better our chances of making a real change.

SHARE YOUR EXPERIENCE

I would LOVE for you to share your transition to becoming an eco-friendly artist with me! Sharing the stories of other artists lists yourself as someone who has made a positive change and is a great way to get more people on board.

GIVE FEEDBACK

Being my first book, I know there is always room for improvement. So, if you have any constructive feedback, please feel free to email me with your suggestions. I would love to re-release this book in a few years' time with your help. And if you know of or use a great eco-friendly art product that I have totally missed, then please let me know so that I can test it and add it into the book.

CORRESPONDING ONLINE VIDEO COURSE

If you are the type of person who learns through visuals, then the online video course version of this book might just be the ticket for you. If you have purchased this book with the video as a package, be sure to check it out.

WORKSHOPS, RETREATS, AND SEMINARS

If you would like me to teach your art group about becoming an eco-friendly artist, you are more than welcome to book me for a weekend workshop, seminar or even an art retreat. I also teach my unique painting techniques and processes and can customise workshops to include both sets of knowledge.

For availability and bookings, please use this form scottdenholm.com/workshops/ or email me at art@scottdenholm.com

MY ART

If you're wondering what my art looks like, then wonder no more! You can find my art on my website and social media.

Website: scottdenholm.com
Instagram: instagram.com/scottdenholm_oceanart/
Facebook: facebook.com/scottdenholm.oceanart/
YouTube: youtube.com/scottdenholmoceanart

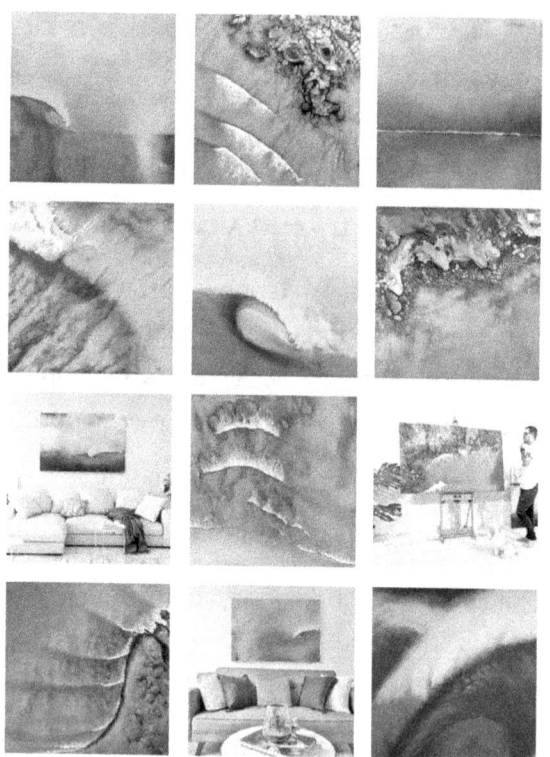

REFERENCES

1. Nontoxic oil painting - an overview, Mike Bergen
   http://www.nontoxichub.com/nontoxicoilpainting

2. Pigment Safety, Angela Babin
   http://www.nontoxichub.com/pigment-safety

3. Hazards and Precautions in Art Painting and Drawing, Art Hazard News, Angela Babin, 1991
   http://www.nontoxichub.com/art-painting-drawing-pigment

4. Art Practice: Goodbye to Turpentine, Robert Maynord, 2012
   https://www.huffpost.com/entry/art-practice-goodbye-to-turpentine_b_1479346

5. Metal Pigments used in Paints and Inks, Center for Safety in The Arts, Various Authors
   http://www.nontoxicprint.com/metalpigments.htm

6. Acrylic Paint
   https://en.wikipedia.org/wiki/Acrylic_paint

7. Thought Co, What Are the Ingredients in Acrylic Paint?, Marion Boddy-Evans
   https://www.thoughtco.com/ingredients-in-acrylic-paint-3976990

8. Safe Painting - Fine Art
   http://www.nontoxicprint.com/safepainting.htm

9. How watercolor paints are made, Bruce MacEvoy, 2018
https://www.handprint.com/HP/WCL/pigmt1.html

10. New World Encyclopedia, Watercolor painting
http://www.newworldencyclopedia.org/entry/Watercolor_painting

11. "Marijuana and Hemp: The Untold Story", Thomas Bouril, 1997
Download the report (PDF: 1.0MB)
https://theartistguide.to/resources/hemp-the-untold-story.pdf

12. Organic Cotton - The risks of cotton farming
https://www.organiccotton.org/oc/Cotton-general/Impact-of-cotton/Risk-of-cotton-farming.php

13. World Wildlife Fund for Nature (WWF) Cotton: a water wasting crop
https://www.worldwildlife.org/industries/cotton

14. World Wildlife Fund for Nature (WWF), Thirsty Crops - Our food and clothes: eating up nature and wearing out the environment?, 2013
https://www.worldwildlife.org/publications/thirsty-crops-our-food-and-clothes-eating-up-nature-and-wearing-out-the-environment

15. World Wildlife Fund for Nature (WWF) Research paper "The impact of cotton on freshwater resources and ecosystems", 1999 Download the paper (PDF: 0.2MB)
https://theartistguide.to/resources/WWF-ImpactOfCotton.pdf

16. PETA, Why Buying an Animal-Hair Paintbrush Is Like Buying Fur, 2017
https://www.peta.org/living/humane-home/animal-friendly-paintbrush-fur-free/

17. National Ocean Service, National Oceanic and Atmospheric Administration, What are micro plastics
https://oceanservice.noaa.gov/facts/microplastics.html

18. National Geographic, Pesky plastic: The true harm of microplastics in the oceans, Jessica Perelman, 2016
https://blog.nationalgeographic.org/2016/04/04/pesky-plastic-the-true-harm-of-microplastics-in-the-oceans/

19. Marine Conservation Society, Ocean Plastic Pollution
https://www.marineconservation.org.au/ocean-plastic-pollution/

20. Cherrett, N., Barrett, J., Clemett, A., Chadwick,M., and Chadwick, M.J. (2005). Ecological Footprint and Water Analysis of Cotton, Hemp and Polyester. Report prepared for and reviewed by BioRegional Development Group and World Wide Fund for Nature – Cymru. SEI Publication. ISBN 91 975238 2 8.
https://www.sei.org/publications/ecological-footprint-water-analysis-cotton-hemp-polyester/
Download the report (PDF: 1.7MB)
https://theartistguide.to/resources/SEI-Report-EcologicalFootprintCottonHempPolyester.pdf

21. University of Newcastle, Australia and Dr Thava Palanisami - Published by World Wide Fund for Nature (WWF) No Plastic In Nature, June 2019
Download the report (PDF: 2.3MB)
https://theartistguide.to/resources/WWF-NoPlasticInNature.pdf

22. European Union - Report from the Commission to the European Parliament and Council - On the impact of the use of oxo-degradable plastic, including oxo-degradable plastic carrier bags, on the environment, 2018
Download the report (PDF: 0.3MB)
https://theartistguide.to/resources/EU-commission-oxo-plastics.pdf

23. Smithsonian Museum Conservation Institute, Determining the Acceptable Ranges of Relative Humidity And Temperature in Museums and Galleries - Part 1, Structural Response to Relative Humidity, Marion F. Mecklenburg, 2016
https://blog.nationalgeographic.org/2016/04/04/pesky-plastic-the-true-harm-of-microplastics-in-the-oceans/

24. Iowa State University - ISU's Soy Research Offers Greener Materials for Hot Wax Art, 2008
https://www.cals.iastate.edu/news/releases/isus-soy-research-offers-greener-materials-hot-wax-art

25. Tong Wang, Linxing Yao. Journal of the American Oil Chemists' Society. Textural and Physical Properties of Biorenewable "Waxes" Containing Partial Acylglycerides, January 2012
https://www.researchgate.net/publication/251397663_Textural_and_Physical_Properties_of_Biorenewable_Waxes_Containing_Partial_Acylglycerides

ABOUT THE AUTHOR

Scott Denholm is an award-winning artist, art tutor, author and photographer. Having been painting since age 10, Scott's unique art journey has led him to become both a successful artist in his own right and a tutor and mentor helping educate many others.

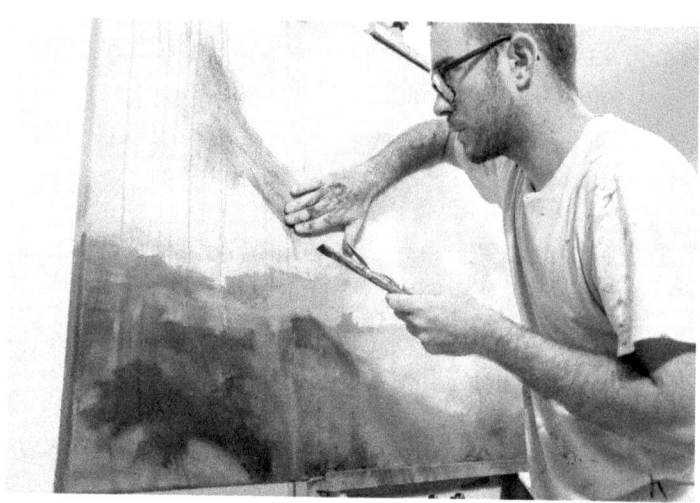

www.ingramcontent.com/pod-product-compliance
Lightning Source LLC
Chambersburg PA
CBHW070245220526
45465CB00004B/1529